POAMORIO

POAMORIO

Darío Canton

Translated from the Spanish by Drew McCord Stroud

with a preface by Jean Franco

SARU Tucson • Tokyo • Buenos Aires

Library of Congress Catalog Card Number: 84-51027
ISBN 0-935086-01-3

PREFACE

Sometime in 1975, I began receiving dark brown envelopes marked **Asemal**. **Asemal** was a letter-poem sent by an Argentine poet and sociologist, Darío Canton. Some of his eight hundred recipients replied to his poems. I myself never did, though the arrival of the brown envelope always seemed like an unexpected gift. It made me nostalgic for the only other venture of the same kind I had ever seen — the old **Corno emplumado** that Margaret Randall and Sergio Mondragón published in Mexico in the sixties. Unlike most literary magazines, **El corno emplumado** not only talked to its readers and printed their replies, but it encouraged the feeling that poetry was not academic fodder, not private heaven, but a unique kind of networking.

Asemal and **El corno emplumado** remind us that poetry does not merely persist like a monument in the modern world, but must find new forms of survival, despite or perhaps because of the postmodern breakdown of genres. The novel has a vast, serialized and often casual readership who owe no particular allegiance to one another. Poetry, on the other hand, seems more closely bound to its readers, who are self-selected in any case.

One kind of Latin American poetry today is a script which can only be realized thru a public reading —such, for instance, is Ernesto Cardenal's recent poetry. At the opposite extreme, there is poetry constructed as a hermeneutic puzzle which requires erudite commentary. **Asemal** represented a third option — the salvaging of communication from such obscenities as the form letter and the rubber-stamped signature. Poems are letters which have no specific destination but invite response.

All Darío Canton's literary work has been characterized by this idiosyncratic confrontation with literary space. The peculiar problem that **Poamorio** poses is how love can be recorded in modern society. There is little in modern Argentina that is not looked at thru the prism of irony and ridicule, and one can hardly think of a topic that invites irony more than sexual love. Perhaps this is because the great modern love poet, Neruda, seemed to be powered by other than mere male,female relationships. One thinks, for instance, of his **Versos de capitán,** the secret poems written under a pseudonym to celebrate his love affair with Matilde Urrutia (whom he later married). There is so much idealized male fantasy in them that the love object seems to become one more excuse for metaphor.

In many Latin American love poems written by men, the poetic "you" is a blank page on which fantasies of creation, conquest and sex are written. This "you" is a paper female, as many women (for instance, Rosario Ferré in her "Fábula de la garza desangrada") have seen.

Not so in Canton's poetry, which grows out of specific moods and situations and avoids the rhetoric, the proliferation of metaphor that comes so easily to Hispanic poets. These poems are spare, often epigrammatic. Like photographs, they capture an exact instant — of triumph, defeat, satisfaction or disappointment. These poems are still monologues — that is, we know only one side of the dialogue. But the "other" is not simply a figment of the imagination. There are two people in this affair.

The poems chart the strategy and tactics of daily encounters in which climax is not the only experience worth remembering. **Poamorio** is thus an attempt to create a non-macho poetry, a poetry that is not oppressive to women. Insofar as it succeeds in doing this, it enters into dialogue with the growing body of gay poetry and poetry by women. Together, these hitherto

marginalized voices promise something new both for
Latin American literature and for sexual politics.

Columbia University

New York City

TRANSLATOR'S NOTE

Poamorio is a pun on the Spanish **poemario**, "a book
of poems." So what is a **poamorio**? It's a book of
poems about love — **amor** — that flows like a river —**río**
— with no end. With unnumbered pages and numbered
poems that begin with 29 "Hamlet" (on the actual front
cover of the original book), they revolve back on them-
selves with 62 (the title page) and then start over again
in medias res with poem 1 "The Truth" and end (on the
original back cover) with 28.

The intent? To portray the multiple affairs of the poet
in their real and imaginary aspects as circular moments
of timeless time. Darío Canton's lovers repeat them-
selves endlessly, cross-examine each other relentless-
ly, reenact all the acts and rituals of love, regale them-
selves, repel each other, retire and then resume. For to
put an end to things would be to die.

No strictly bordered male or female is outlined here,
as couples detect parts of themselves becoming the
prohibited other, master becoming slave, or both
merging Siamese in mutual infatuation. Like a river, love
can carry the poet out of his natural shape and run
away with him.

This translation evolved out of a long correspondence
with the poet. We are both bilingual, so the translation

is nearly as much the poet's work as my own, and it has gone thru countless transcontinental drafts. I have tried to make each poem stand as an English poem in its own right, and as my poem. But I have occasionally yielded a lyric impulse or two to the author's superior claims.

I owe our acquaintance to our mutual friend, the Mexican poet Enrique González González. And to Richard W. Weatherhead, Douglas W. Schwartz and the Witter Bynner Foundation for Poetry, my thanks for making this publication possible.

DREW McCORD STROUD

University of Arizona

Tucson

Table of Contents

POAMORIO

A la que ama con frescura

y es mujer que exige hombría

29 Sostengo tu calavera
contra mi boca
te dejo hacer
mi macho
mientras juegas a serlo
y te enojas
revierto los papeles
y sobre ti bajo
como una madre me recibes
abierta

29 *I hold your skull*
against my mouth
and let you be
my man
while you play at being one
and get turned on
I switch parts
and go down on you
like a mother you take me
open wide

30

Los libros lo declaran:
debe olvidar el amante
si el amor ha fracasado
olvidar
completamente
—capítulo cinco, b.

Pero yo
que voy mirando
hacia el suelo
cuando ando preocupado
que capto
las miradas que se cruzan
y el oscuro recorrido
de los jugos en el vientre
sostengo
que hay libros
no escritos todavía
hijos por nacer
sangre
sangre corriendo
vida

30

It says in books:
lovers must forget
if love has failed
forget
completely
—chapter five, b.
But as for me
I go around with
my eyes on the ground
when I'm upset
I capture
the looks that cross each other
the dark reconnoitering
of the juices of the gut
And I submit
that there are books
still unwritten
children yet unborn
blood
blood running
life

maravillosa

abierta

rota

marvelous
broken
red

31

Crece el cuerpo
se expande
en la medida
en que me faltas.
Tienes que venir
a sujetarlo
volverlo a sus contornos
antes que de mí se escape

31 *The body grows*
it fills
to fit
the places where you fail me.
You have to come
to take it back
to its natural shape
before it runs away from me

Acta

32 Por la presente doy fe
a quien pueda interesar
y a los fines pertinentes
que yo gocé del amor
me retiré satisfecho
en dos o veinte ocasiones.

En prueba de lo cual firmo
este único ejemplar

Certificate

32   *I hereby state*
to whom it may concern
and for the purposes at hand
that I rejoiced in love
withdrawing satisfied
on two or twenty occasions.

In confirmation of said fact, I sign
this single-volume limited edition

El orden

33 Acaso es mejor
que no te encuentre
ahora
si estás tan apurada.
El polvo de los muebles
sacudido cada día
el trapo que se pasa
por el piso
hasta dejarlo brillante
son todas cosas muy dignas
de salvación

33 *Maybe it's better*
not to meet
now
you're in such a rush.
The dust from the furniture
wiped off each day
the rag that's run
across the floor
until it's shining
are all things
worthy of salvation

34 El perro
no puede vivir
sin tu cariño
te busca
por los cuartos
de la casa
gime desolado.
Espera
por las noches
tu regreso
amanece
tiritando
al lado
del lugar
en que dormías
come poco
desmejora
extraña
tu mano
y alimento.
Mi cuerpo

34
The dog
can't live
without your love
he looks
in all the rooms
of the house
for you
howls in desolation.
Waits
at night
for your return
wakes up
shivering
beside
the place
you used to sleep
he barely eats
he's looking bad
he misses
your hand
and food.
My body

35 Ahora
que te has ido
llevándote tu cuerpo
puedo mentir:
nunca nadie me ha querido
como me quisiste vos

35 *Now*
that you've gone
taking your body with you
I can lie:
no one ever loved me
like you loved me

La compañía

36   **Como tocar el cuerpo de otro**
desconocido
en el tanteo del que explora
y se pregunta
cuáles las leyes del juego
así me toco
extraño
remoto
reconozco
—un hombre
un hombre
estoy seguro;
alcanzo a vislumbrar
que nada importa el sexo
sino

36   *The way you touch*
the body of another
stranger
feeling your way
asking yourself
what are the rules of the game
that's how I touch myself
strange
distant
I recognize
—a man
a man
I'm sure;
I finally get the idea
sex makes no difference
only

37

Un eco extraño
adentro
y una voz terca
que dice
se acabó, se acabó
y lo sigue repitiendo.

No recuerdo cuándo fue.

EL CUADRO

SE MOVIO DE SU LUGAR.

Seguimos celebrando
al amor
citándole
en nuestra casa
dándole entrada
en el cuarto.
Pero ya no era como antes.

37

A peculiar echo
inside
and a stubborn voice
that says
it's over, it's over
and keeps repeating it.

I don't remember when.

THE PICTURE
WAS MOVED FROM ITS PLACE.

We kept on celebrating
love
receiving him
at our place
letting him into
the room.
But it wasn't like it used to be.

NADIE LO VIO; NI NOSOTROS

Me miro en el espejo
veo el cuerpo, gigantesco
y un rostro deforme
monstruoso.
Recorro las calles
regreso de noche
muy tarde.
En la oscuridad
respiras;
no te veo.
Los dos cerca
separados.

Llamamos a los amigos
hacemos una gran fiesta
les pedimos que nos den
el ejemplo de sus vidas.

Se dan vuelta
avergonzados.

**NOBODY NOTICED;
NOT EVEN US.**

I look at myself in the mirror
I see the body, gigantic
and a deformed
monster face.
I walk the streets
and return
late at night.
You breathe
in the darkness;
I don't see you.
The two so near
apart.

We call our friends
we put on a big party
and ask them to give us
the example of their lives.

They turn
in shame.

EL BARCO SE SEPARA
DEL MUELLE LENTAMENTE.

Sacerdotes atildados
del culto del dios vienés
contestan nuestro llamado
escuchan con atención
—lo espero el próximo lunes
a las seis y media
en punto:
el curarse está en sus manos

INFORMAN POR LA RADIO
QUE LAS AGUAS
DE LOS MARES
VAN BAJANDO
LOS MASTILES DEJAN VER
DE NAVIOS MUY ANTIGUOS.

Concurro a las bibliotecas
permanezco todo el día:
me entero cómo se muere
rechaza
cómo se elige y engendra

THE BOAT SLOWLY
PARTS FROM THE DOCK.

Fashion plate priests
of the cult of the Viennese god
answer our call
listen attentively
—I'll be waiting for you
next Monday
at six thirty
on the dot:
the cure is in your hands

THEY SAY ON THE RADIO
THAT THE WATERS
OF THE SEAS
ARE GOING DOWN
THE MASTS CAN BE SEEN
OF VERY OLD SHIPS.

I go off to the libraries
stay all day:
I get to know how one dies
rejects
how one opts for and engenders

cuándo se debe decir
sí o no
ahora, más tarde o nunca.

ATARDECE EN EL BARRIO
SACA UN VIEJO SU SILLA
A LA VEREDA.

En la noche
despierto a tu lado
me devuelvo el sexo;
coloco el reloj en la muñeca
salgo
cierro la puerta con cuidado.

EL BARCO ACABA DE ZARPAR
SE ESCUCHAN MAS LEJANOS
LOS ADIOSES.

Yo camino
acelero el paso
corro

when one is to say
yes or no
now, later or never.

IT'S GETTING DARK IN THE
NEIGHBORHOOD
AN OLD MAN TAKES HIS CHAIR
OUT TO THE SIDEWALK.

At night
I wake up at your side
and recover my sex;
I put on my wristwatch
I go out
and shut the door with care.

THE BOAT HAS JUST WEIGHED
ANCHOR
THE GOODBYES
CAN BE HEARD IN THE DISTANCE.

I start walking
walk faster
run

38

Es útil cada tanto
medir las tensiones
de los hilos que nos unen:
los cables de acero
las telarañas
soportan almas
de distinto peso

38 *It's useful every now and then*
to gauge the tension
of the threads that bind us:
steel cables
spiderwebs
hold up souls
of different weights

39 La muerte que me infliges
repentina
era de esperar.
Huelo a justo
y ése es
después de todo
mal olor

39 *The death you*
suddenly
inflict on me
might be expected.
I come up
smelling like roses
a foul smell
after all

40

Es un rasgo
de civilizado entendimiento
saber decir adiós
echar a caminar
al mismo tiempo
en distintas direcciones
duelo de truhanes
que no giran
cuando deben
y provocan la risa
al salir de la escena

40

It is a mark
of civilized behavior
to know how to say goodbye
to go off walking
at the same time
in different directions
two comics paired off
who don't swing
when they ought to
and give everyone a laugh
as they slip from the scene

Curiosidad

41
Ha de ser difícil
pienso
saber
los hombres que has conocido
a menos que te pregunte
y no quiero
—podría resultar tedioso.
No sé por qué este deseo
de reconstruir
tu himen virgen
si ya nadie
se precia
de tenerlo

41

It must be difficult
I guess
to know
the men you've known
except by asking you
and I don't want to
—it could turn out to be a drag.
I don't understand this urge
to reconstruct
your virgin hymen
if no one
thinks it's worth
having any more

Del amor

42   Lo que la gente quiere
muy sencillo
es que la quieran;
pero eso
naturalmente
no se impone
o en caso de imponerse
alcanza
duraciones limitadas

42 *What people want*
is quite simple:
to be wanted
but that
of course
cannot be made to happen
or if it can
prevails
for only a limited time

Carta

43 Me separo de tí
dulce amada
lamentando
el fragmento de arco
que falta a tu
circunferencia
las notas del registro
que te hubieran permitido
llegar al do sobreagudo.

Espero
deseo
no dudo
podrás
completar tu formación
harás feliz
a más de un hombre

Letter

43 *I split off from you*
sweet belovéd
mourning
the section of the arc
missing from your
circumference
the notes of the register
that would have permitted
you to reach high C.
I hope
I wish
I don't doubt
you'll be able
to round out your education
you'll make
more than one man happy

44 Ahora
mientras miro
cómo el segundero
marca los latidos
y pienso si será
si volverás
espero tu decisión
busco los conjuros
de la magia
los brebajes encantados
el ritual de los espejos;
siento
que haría cualquier cosa
cambiar de nombre
rostro
alma
por no estar solo

44

Now
while I watch
the second hand
tick off its heartbeats
and wonder will it happen
will you come back
I wait for your decision
and look to conjure up
an ancient spell
the witches' brew
the mirror ritual:
I feel
I might do anything
change my name
face
soul
just not to be alone

45 El combate se repite
otra vez
con todo el estruendo
entrechocar de cuerpos
olor a sangre
descarga de la metralla
golpe que retumba del cañón

Hay que repetirlo
para que se advierta
que no es el mismo
sólo un simulacro

45 *The battle breaks out*
once more
with all its clamor
the clash of bodies
the scent of blood
machine-guns' hammering
a shot that echoes from the cannon

It has to be done again
to warn them
it's not the real thing
it's just for the movies

46 Nosotros
que aquí estamos
callados
quietos
o hablamos largamente
quietos
sin que jamás pase nada
¿aprenderemos
que el reino de la muerte
incluye eso
quietud?

46 *Those of us*
who here are
quiet
still
or speak at length
still
with nothing happening at all
will we learn
that the kingdom of death
includes that
stillness?

47 Aprendices
en el arte sin testigos
puertas
que se abren
sin golpear
calles
que juntos recorremos
armando la ciudad
poblándola
hasta que colmada
maestros
la destruimos

47   *Apprentices*
of the art without witnesses
doors
that open
without knocking
streets
we walk together
setting up the city
populating it
until, sated
we, masters
destroy it

48 En medio del fragor
de las máquinas
nos amamos.
No nos oíamos
recurrimos
a papeles
pizarras mágicas
era complicado
engorroso
utilizamos
micrófonos
altoparlantes
enredamos en los cables

Tiempo después
tuvimos un tornillo

48

Amid the roar
of the machines
we made love.
We couldn't hear ourselves talk
we resorted
to little notes
magic slates
it was a nuisance
trying
we used
microphones
loudspeakers
got tangled up in cables

A little later
A screw was born

49

El amor
gran pájaro de fuego
se ha posado otra vez
sobre nosotros:
nos bate con sus alas
duras
guarda la puerta
hace de nos
otros dioses
que socavan los cimientos
febril, tranquilamente
seguros como la marea
incesante
que fluye y que refluye
mientras es

49

Love
that great firebird
has settled once again
upon us:
he fans us with his
stiff wings
guarding the door
he makes of us
other gods
that hollow out the foundations
feverishly, languidly
secure as the tide
unceasingly
coming and going
as long as it's there

50

Prescindo
de tus partes blandas
acaricio tu sólido pie
promontorio pequeño
resistente
recorro la tibia
me detengo en la rodilla
pomo de la espada
juego con la rótula
presiono
salto a la cadera
busco sus límites
palpo tus costillas
desordenada
duramente.
Los indios lo sabían:
el frote de palillos
rápido
delgados
es un modo

Bony Eroticism

50

I can do without
your soft parts
I caress your durable foot
tough little peak
I run along your tibia
I pause at the knee
pommel of the sword
I play with your kneecap
press it in
leap to the hip
search out its limits
probe the ribs
wildly
roughly.
The Indians knew how:
rubbing thin sticks
rapidly
together
is one way

51

se eleva
deslumbrante
el hongo
sobre el atolón
soles soles soles
machimbre
machimbre
machimbre
me acoplo
hago el cambio de vías
fluyen por el tubo
leche aceite
presiono
amaso tus tetas
hacia mí
Te tiro de las piernas

51 *The mushroom The mushroom*
dazzling dazzling
rises rises
over the atoll over the atoll
suns suns suns suns suns suns
coupling coupling
coupling coupling
coupling coupling
I switch tracks I switch tracks
flow thru the tube flow thru the tube
milk oil milk oil
I press I press
I knead I knead
your tits your tits
towards me towards me
I pull you by the legs I pull you by the legs

52

La entrega
de tu cuerpo
no me engaña:
quiero el alma
el alma
las monedas
que ocultas temerosa

52   *The surrender*
of your body
doesn't fool me:
I want your soul
the soul
the coins
you hoard in fear

53 En medio de la noche
excitado
me despierto
echo sobre vos
como un caballo levanto
desbocado
con mis cascos
la tierra de tus sueños

53 *I wake up*
excited
in the middle of the night
I throw myself on you
like a runaway horse
my hooves kick up
the soil of your dreams

54 Salgo de tu fuego
purificado
me devuelvo al que era;
puedo callar
ahora
como aquél que estuvo
y sabe

54   *I emerge from your fire*
purified
I return to what I was:
I can keep my silence
now
like the one who was there
and knows

Final

55 **Todos los gestos**
de la buena voluntad
fueron cumplidos
las atenciones
en los días señalados
lo debido a cada uno
el peso exacto
el orden de precedencia
todo fue hecho
calculado
respetado

hasta el hastío

Finale

55 *All the gestures*
of goodwill
were performed
attention
on the designated days:
what each one was owed
the exact measure
the order of precedence
everything was done
with calculation
with respect

and with loathing

56 GENERAL CONSTERNACION:
PERDEMOS EN EL ESPACIO
VOS Y YO.

Maniobras previstas
ensayadas en tierra
fracasan.

Fallas técnicas
aún no localizadas
desvían
de los cursos trazados
impiden acople.

Se preven
para el futuro
vuelos sin tripulación

56 ***GENERAL CONSTERNATION:***
LOST IN SPACE
YOU AND I.
Prearranged maneuvers
tested on earth
aborted.
Technical failures
still unlocated
deviations
from the prepared course
prevent linkup.
It is predicted
that future missions
will be unmanned

57

Te araño
la cara de goma
mentida
te clavo los dedos
te cavo canales
te saco la sangre
corriendo a raudales
te rompo la cara
la cara
la mirada torva
te parto
metiendo el cuchillo
lo hundo y lo saco
lo hundo y lo saco
tu concha cobija caín
cantando con cara
de culo cansado
canción sepulcral.
Las rosas
no alcanzan
todo aquello rojo
que quise llevarte

57

I claw
at your rubber face
pretender
I dig in my fingers
I carve you open
I drain your blood
running in torrents
I smash your face
your face
your fierce glare
I dispel
with a knife
I thrust it in and pull it out
I thrust it in and pull it out
your cunt gives Cain a cover
singing with screwed-up smile
sepulchral songs.
There aren't
roses enough
to give you
all the red
I wanted to bring you

para coronar la mierda
masa cenagosa
chupando hacia adentro
cogiendo crueldad

to crown
the muddy mass of shit
sucking up from inside
screwing cruelly

Amo

58 **Doblado sobre el piso**
lamo tus zapatos;
doblado sobre el piso
lamo tus zapatos;
doblado sobre el piso
lamo tus zapatos;
lamo tus zapatos
lamo tus zapatos
lamo tus zapatos;
el chorro de tu orín
no cae;
el chorro de tu orín
no cae
no cae
no cae;
tus tetas no bajan
tus tetas redondas
no bajan, no bajan, no bajan;
tus ojos miran adelante
sé;
tus ojos miran adelante
sé

58 *Doubled up on the floor*
I lick your shoes;
doubled up on the floor
I lick your shoes;
doubled up on the floor
I lick your shoes;
I lick your shoes
I lick your shoes
I lick your shoes;
the trickle of your piss
doesn't fall;
the trickle of your piss
doesn't fall
doesn't fall
doesn't fall;
your tits don't reach me
your bulbous tits
don't reach me, reach me,
reach me;
your eyes look straight ahead
I know;
your eyes look straight ahead
I know

lamo tus zapatos
lamo tus zapatos
lamo tus zapatos
rozo tus empeines
rozo tus empeines
rozo tus empeines
lamo tus zapatos
rozo tus empeines
lamo tus zapatos
rozo tus empeines
lamo tus zapatos
rozo tus empeines
lamo tus zapatos
lamo tus zapatos

Sobre el piso
doblado
no alzo la cabeza
no alzo la cabeza
no alzo la cabeza
no alzo la cabeza
no alzo

I lick your shoes
I lick your shoes
I lick your shoes
I nibble at your instep
I nibble at your instep
I nibble at your instep
I lick your shoes
I nibble at your instep
I lick your shoes
I nibble at your instep
I lick your shoes
I nibble at your instep
I lick your shoes
I lick your shoes

On the floor
doubled up
I don't lift up my head
I don't lift up my head
I don't lift up my head
I don't lift up my head
I don't lift up

59 La riqueza
con que estábamos vestidos
los detalles relucientes
ceremonial de la alabanza
en que morosamente
nos complacíamos
mirada recorriendo
las curvas
de la manga
su caída
la forma
en que estaban
pegados los botones
el corte de la solapa
el tono de la tela
y sus reflejos
de noche y de día
toda esa luz
resplandor
perdidos.

Deshilachados

59

The richness
with which we were clothed
the glittering detail
the rite of eulogy
on which we lavished
our attentions
the glance following
the curves
of the sleeve
its fall
the way
the buttons
were attached
the cut of the lapel
the hue of the material
and what it reflected
by night and day
all that light
brilliance
lost

Unraveled

raídos
hechos trizas
pobres otra vez

threadbare
ripped to shreds
poor once more

60

Aún recuerdo
cómo nos amamos
ese día
su acabar incontable
y mi deseo
cada vez más crecido
sin encontrar el modo
mi sexo
fuera de toda proporción
sin salida
y ella
satisfecha
gritando de dolor
mientras yo
turbado
no sabía cómo volver
a la normalidad
era imposible
siameses por el sexo
ligados
nos llevaron a Europa

60

I still remember
how we loved
that day
her unaccountable comings
and my desire
each time greater
without having found a way
my sex
out of all proportion
with no way out
and she
satisfied
screaming with pain
while I
bewildered
did not know how to go back
to normal
it was impossible
made Siamese by sex
attached together
they carried us to Europe

los Estados Unidos
al fin nos separaron
con unas inyecciones
nuevas
dudaban
pero dieron resultado
nos volvimos
por distintas vías
temblando
de sólo recordar
estremecidos
ante el temor

Después ya nunca
fuimos los mismos

and America
at last they separated us
with new injections
doubting the outcome
but it worked
we came home
by different routes
trembling
just to think of it
shuddering
in fear

Afterwards we were
never again the same

61 Tome una hoja
de papel en blanco
a altas horas
de la noche
y con una lapicera
preferentemente azul
comience a escribir
el nombre
que corresponda
de izquierda a derecha
renglón por renglón
renglón por renglón
hasta que la mano
agotada
haga trazos
ilegibles.
Después fume
un cigarrillo
—si no fuma
puede dar
una vuelta

61
Take a sheet
of blank paper
late in the evening
and with a ball-pen
preferably blue
begin to write
the name
that corresponds
from left to right
line by line
line by line
until the hand
exhausted
leaves illegible
marks.
Afterwards
smoke a cigarette
—if you don't smoke
you can take
a walk

a la manzana—
apague la radio
desvístase
cuidadosamente
y métase
en la cama
tratando de asegurar
que al dormirse
la cabeza apunte
hacia el noroeste.
A la mañana siguiente
después del desayuno
recomience

around the block—
turn off the radio
take off your clothes
carefully
and get into bed
trying to make sure
that when you fall asleep
your head points
to the northwest.
On the following morning
after breakfast
start all over again

62 Poamorio

Do
de
ca
den
cia
fó
ni
ca
cuan
do
de
ca
e
a
mor
mue
re

62 Poamorio

Do
re
mi
ni
sense
phone
tick
when
I don't
a
do
re
you
any
more
you
die

La verdad

1

**Quien se acuesta contigo
y te abraza
y te besa
y llega hasta el final
no soy yo**

The Truth

1   *Who lies with you*
and puts his arms around you
and kisses you
and comes right to the end
is not me

2   Bajé a la cueva:
tanteé
sus cuatro paredes
y el techo bajo.
Me dije:
aquí no viviría

Me quedé

2

I went down into the cave:
felt
its four walls
and low ceiling
I told myself:
I couldn't live here

I stayed

3 **El cigarrillo**
el cigarrillo encendido
que yo te apagué en la mano
voló como serpentina.

Tu grito quedó en el aire.
Yo me fui a curar la herida

3

The cigarette
the lighted cigarette
I put out for you
in your hand
flew up like a paper streamer.

Your scream stayed in the air.
I went to fix my wound

4   Si la libertad
no tengo
de asesinarte
¿cómo me pides que te ame?

4 *If I'm*
not free
to assassinate you
how can you ask me to love you?

Diálogo

5
      La mano sabe
que el cuerpo
necesita compañía
y tierna y sostenida
lo acompaña.
La mano entiende
—es uno de los puentes—
y calla
juró guardar silencio;
la mente sabe igual
es zorra vieja
que todo es un engaño
pero nada dice

Dialogue

5

The hand knows
that the body
needs company
and tenderly, supportively
stays with it.
The hand understands
—it is one of the bridges—
and is silent
it swore to keep silent;
the mind knows too
that all is deception
it's an old fox
but it says nothing

6

Yo
que fuera amante
cómo contar
este fracaso
vacuo ahora
cantarlo
decir que no me huelgo
radiante
con abrazos.
Yo
que hice voto
de simiente compartida
me encuentro
ante un dilema
que enfrentan los poetas:

¿inventaré una amante?

6

I
who was once a lover
how can I face
this failure now
empty how can I
sing it
say I won't lie at ease
glowing
in embraces.
I
who took a vow
of shared semen
find myself
in the dilemma
that confronts poets:

shall I invent a lover?

7

Deliberadamente
pensando en ella
compré preservativos
y los guardé en el bolsillo.
Después nos encontramos
como dos buenos amigos
y sin más misterio
decidimos acostarnos.
Es lo que corresponde
al fin y al cabo
entre seres
de distinto sexo.

La multitud
congregada a la salida
aplaudió.
Cualquiera hubiera dicho
se trataba
de la pareja
presidencial

7

Deliberately
thinking about her
I bought some safes
and kept them in my pocket.
Later we met
like two old friends
and with no further to-do
decided to go to bed.

It's what should happen
after all
between persons
of separate sexes.

The crowd
applauded
congregated at the exit.
Any bystander
would have said
we were
President
and First Lady

8

Apremiado
por urgencias que conozco
distante
cortés
eficiente
como cuchillo
aunque no corte
hiero.

—Mujer
¿te parece bien ahora?

8

Prodded by urges
I'm familiar with
distant
courteous
efficient
like a knife
though I don't cut
I wound.

—Woman
is it all right now?

9

Tu cuerpo
indefinido todavía
en la aurora del camino
que recién se bifurca
tu ser
que busca vagamente
encontrarse en otros rostros
como un ciego
con certeza tienta
palpa
lentamente
no se aturde
criminal
tras su máscara de imbécil
como roca se desprende
pesada
de lo alto
dando tumbos
sabe que no irá
no podrá ir
más allá del valle
me recorre

9

Your body
still undefined
at sunrise on the road
that recently divided
your being
that vaguely searches
to find itself in others' faces
like a blind man
feels his way unerringly
gropes along
gradually
never bewildered
nefarious
behind its idiot mask
like a rock loosening itself
heavily
from a height
tumbling
it knows it won't go
knows it can't go
beyond the valley
it goes over me

registra
insiste
no me deja
termina por encontrar.

Juro que soy inocente
que sólo fui un instrumento.
Eso sí
desde ya te autorizo
a que me nombres
en tus futuras Memorias

inspects
persists
won't let me
finds it at last.

I swear I'm innocent
They only used me.
I grant you my permission
though
to use my name in print
in your forthcoming Memoirs

10

Amagas
amenazas
corro el riesgo del destierro
el émbolo se desliza
libre
sin fricción
el límite la cabeza
llega hasta el punto
y no sale
se interna
llega hasta el punto
y no sale
juego que absorbe
manejas con maestría
sostienes
alientas con tu perfume
hasta que verdugo subes
segura los escalones
lanzas la cuchilla

10

You threaten
you menace
I run the risk of exile
the piston slips along
freely
without friction
the limit's the head
it reaches the end
and doesn't come out
it goes in deep
it reaches the end
and doesn't come out
a movement that absorbs
you operate skillfully
sustain
encourage with your scent
until, executioner, you mount
the steps assuredly
allow the blade to fall

decapitas
artificio
máquina de los hombres
roto
deshecha la torre
la marea
se la lleva

decapitate

broken

artifact

the male instrument

the tower shattered

the tide

takes it away

11   Petróleo
regando el contorno
manguera desatada
cuando tu boca

11 *Oil*
sprinkling all around
a reeling hose
whenever your mouth

12 Bloque esta noche
tu cuerpo
recto.
Geométrico te amo
hago el juego a que me obligas
—abrazo riguroso
preciso
modelo de economía
erótico mecánica

12 *Your body*
is a concrete block
tonight.
I love you geometrically
I play by your rules
—rigorous embrace
precise
a model of erotic
and mechanical economy

13 Eternizarse
en el duende de tu sexo
el mío quiere;
no se puede
le digo
se escuchan los pasos
lejanos
pero ciertos

13　*To eternalize itself*
in the unearthliness of your sex
is what mine wants:
it can't
I tell it
footfalls are heard
far off
but determined

14 Porque
si trato de verme
desnudo
durmiendo junto a vos
sintiendo tu carne dura
firme
la respiración
pausada
anhelante
porque si bajo hasta el fondo
tanteando en la oscuridad
reconociendo los rostros
la boca a la que unirnos
qué encuentro
si no el buscar, buscar;

porque si pienso además
cómo te dormías
cansada
sobre el piso
cómo tu cuerpo buscaba
mi calor para abrigarse

14 *Because*
if I try to look at myself
in the nude
sleeping next to you
feeling your hard flesh
firm
the breathing
steady
yearning
because if I go down to the bottom
groping in darkness
taking note of the faces
the mouth we could hook up with
what do I find
if not searching, searching

because if I think also
of how you used to sleep
exhausted
on the floor
how your body would look for
my heat to warm itself

y escucho al lado
los ruidos de la noche
y luego la claridad
insinuarse, venir
la vida es un gran tronco
que corre río abajo
con vos allí
sobre la alfombra
durmiendo
y todo ha quedado quieto
salvo el corazón
y yo, despierto
despierto, velo
qué encuentro
si no el buscar, buscar

La magia de la vida que se acaba

and hear next door
the sounds of the night
and then the light
insinuate itself, arrive
life is a big log
that drifts downstream
with you there
on the carpet
sleeping
and everything has gone still
except my heart
and I, awake
wide awake, I watch
what do I find
if not searching, searching

The miracle of life
that comes to an end

Mantis religiosa

15   **Cabeza de vaca tu rostro**
asiento pulido;
hilos alambrados
muy blancos y negros
caen desde un centro.
Mirar sostenido
sin mezcla, desvío
trayecto que juntos recorren
tus ojos y brazos
—las palas se alzan
se mueven sin ruido
largas me rodean
aprietan.

Yo cubro tu vientre en silencio:
el sacrificio

Praying Mantis

15 *Your face a cow's head*
a polished seat:
wired filaments
very black and white
fall from a center.
Sustained
unswerving gaze
synchronized trajectory
of eyes and arms
—your blades ascend
they move without a sound
they aim for me
they seize.

I cover your belly in silence:
the sacrifice

16 La piel la reconozco:
he visto similares
en vitrinas de museos.
La beso
mientras me acaricias
me pregunto
si las huellas
de los labios quedarán
serán vistas
con las lupas del futuro
en los vapores
de abrazos
y huecos de tu cuerpo

16 The skin I recognize:
similar ones I've seen
in glass cases in museums.
I kiss it
while you caress me
I ask myself
if traces
will remain
of lips
for the magnifying glasses
of the future
in the haze
of embraces
and hollows of your body

17   Aquí
ahora
no digas más;
hacélo
hacélo

17 *Here*
now
say no more;
do it
do it

18 Dentro de tu orgasmo
el mío
encerrado
y los gritos de los dos
confundidos
sobre la pared del tiempo

18 *Inside your orgasm*
mine
locked up
and the cries of the two
mingled
on the wall of time

19
El guerrero
coloca su armadura:
montó de noche
la guarda de las armas
se dirige
hacia el campo de batalla.
Entra al recinto
y saluda:
será el que inicie el combate.
Suave.
constante
en los flancos
en el centro
a retaguardia.
El otro no cede;
agita y calla.
Es su turno ahora:
ataca sutilmente
provoca
entre nada y algo
la distancia explora
el matiz exacto.

19 *The warrior*
dons his armor:
all night he kept
the vigil
he turns
towards the field of battle.
He enters the precinct
and salutes:
he shall be the one
to start the combat.
Smooth
constant
on the flanks
in the center
at the rear.
The other one doesn't give in:
unrelenting and silent.
It's his turn now:
his subtle attack
pokes
between something and nothing
explores the distance
the exact nuance.

Sin heridas.
Vuelve el guerrero inicial
a probar suerte
busca, embiste
muerde, aprieta
a pie firme
sin un paso.

Ya están
los dos
cuerpo a cuerpo
luchando fieramente
ruedan
por el suelo
se aquietan
como un río de lo alto
bajan
concertados
en medio de los gritos
y el concurso
de los espejos

Unwounded.
The first warrior
tries his luck again
he checks, then he charges
he bites, he closes in
feet firmly on the ground
without giving an inch.

Now
the two
are locked in combat
fighting furiously
they roll
on the ground
they grow still:
like a river
they fall from a height
come to terms
among the shouts
before the mirrors

20   Tus pechos
planta escasa
los riego y acaricio
Mitad casi muchacho
en el comienzo
húmeda, tan tibia
si te busco más abajo
ambivalente, anfibia
como prohibido masculino
atraes
con certidumbre de mujer te das
ritual
desbordando mis lados

20 *Your breasts*
sparse crop
I water and caress them.
Half like a boy's
at the start
humid, so warm
if I search farther down
ambivalent, amphibian
like prohibited male
you attract me
with the certitude of woman
you render
ritual
overflowing my sides

El amor de la forma

21   **Puesto que estoy enamorado**
y ahora, casualmente
leo poemas
con todos los nombres propios
Magdalena, Estela, Margarita
devotas dedicatorias
fijadas, limitadas
me prometo desde ya
no nombrarte
hacer que mis poemas
te sean fieles de otro modo

21

Since I am in love
and now, casually
read poems
with all the proper names
Magdalena, Stella, Marguerite
fixed, delimited
devoted dedications
I promise myself
from this moment
not to name you
to arrange for my poems
to be faithful to you
after another fashion

Cuando yo no

22 **Como trompo**
te lanzo por el aire
y caes
sobre el piso
bailarina
con mi impulso
girando

When I Don't

22

Like a spinning top
I hurl you through the air
and you fall
on the ground
ballerina
turning
on my impulse

23   Si lo mismo que te hago
otro te hiciera
qué de mí quedaría
me pregunto
a no ser el vacío.
Tu grito
en mis oídos:
cogéme, cogéme

23 *If someone else did it*
the same way I do it
what would be left of me
I ask myself
besides a vacuum.
Your cry
on my ears:
fuck me, fuck me

24 Un hombre enciende el cigarrillo
sentado, lejos
detrás del vidrio.
El piano toca
notas sueltas
armando la melodía.
Estoy en equilibrio
contenido
más abajo de mí mismo
sabiendo que no puedo
queriendo hacerlo
sabiendo sin embargo
que el trato
entre dos seres
—es el pacto—
se agota en el momento
que nada
hay que pedir
ni agradecer
que lo que yo te he dado
y vos me has dado
es lo previsto

24 Far off
sitting behind the partition
a man is lighting a cigarette.
The piano plays
random notes
building the melody.
I am in equilibrium
self-contained
deep inside
knowing I can't
but wanting to do it
knowing nonetheless
that the relation
between two people
—it's the agreement—
is exhausted the moment
that there's nothing
left to ask
nor to be grateful for
that what I have given you
and you have given me
is only what's to be expected

que vos no sos de mí
ni yo de vos
que todo intento de unirnos
deberá ser hecho a un lado
que tenemos un camino
cada uno
un largo camino a recorrer
que nadie habita
en los bares
ni duerme en las esquinas
que siempre se vuelve
por las noches
a la soledad del cuarto
a contar
las paredes y recuerdos
guardarlos en el cajón
tiernamente ordenarlos
con el resto de equilibrio
que nos quede
plenos de amor vencido
mendigos del encuentro
que rompa los caminos

that you aren't mine
and I'm not yours
that any attempt to unite
will have to be set aside
that we have a road
each one
a long road to travel
that nobody lives
in bars
or sleeps on street corners
that they always go home
at night
to the solitude of their rooms
to count
the walls and memories
put them away in the drawer
tenderly arrange them
with the rest of the equilibrium
that is left to us
replete with defeated love
beggars for meetings
that will end lonely roads

expectables y expectantes

los cabellos bien peinados

con alcohol en las venas

con humo en las venas

sin sangre en las venas

dispuestos

esperando

esta noche como vos

alguien, algo

dos caminos

esperando

el momento del encuentro

sonreír

amarnos

dormir en el engaño

decirnos luego adiós

dos caminos

porque vos sos así

y yo lo soy

irremediables

cada uno con lo suyo

sin poderlo compartir

respectable and expectant
the hair well combed
with alcohol in the veins
with smoke in the veins
with no blood in the veins
willing
waiting
this night like you
someone, something
two roads
awaiting
the moment of the encounter
smile
love each other
sleep on the deception
later say goodbye
two roads
because you are this way
and I am so
beyond help
each one on his own
unable to share it

porque vos no estás hecha
con madera del amor
y encuentros
son sólo encuentros
y un abrazo
es lo mismo que otro abrazo
porque si todo se acaba
qué sentido tiene
la torre que el tiempo venza
si es mejor
equilibrados
no alterar
el fiel de la balanza
y unirnos
decir adiós
ahora
que al piano se agregan voces
y el hombre
ya tira el cigarrillo

because you aren't made

from such stuff as love is

and meetings

are only meetings

and one embrace

is the same as another

*because if everything comes
to an end*

what sense does it make

the tower to conquer time

if it's better

on balance

not to alter

the needle on the scale

and to come together

say goodbye

now

that voices

are joining in with the piano

and the man

*is already tossing his cigarette
away*

25

Jinete
te rodeo
con mis brazos
y mis piernas
siento la fuerza de tu cuerpo
que entra y sale
entra y sale
vaivén que me sacude
excita, altera
hasta que llega el triunfo
y te deshago
te mato adentro mío
la madre vuelvo a ser
que te acaricia
tierna
cuando lloras

25

My rider
I throw
my arms
around you
and my legs
I feel your body's force
that enters and exits
enters and exits
a swinging that shakes me
excites and upsets
until victory comes
and I unload you
I kill you deep inside me
I'm a mother again
and I caress you
tenderly
while you cry

26

Crucificada a mí
horizontal
galopas a escape
mas no huyes
el clavo que te unía
fundes
liberas
jadeante me retiro
tras los ayes

26 *Crucified against me*
horizontally
you gallop away
but don't make your break
the nail that joined you
you fuse
you set me free
throbbing I retreat
behind my moans

La perfección

27

I
Encuentros
de tu carne y de la mía
constante embate
brazos
y piernas
y besos sucedidos
y siempre tu cabeza
girando
y yo con ella

II
Dioses
que miden sus fuerzas
observan, en silencio
escultores su obra
nosotros
labrándonos los cuerpos
pisando con certeza
los peldaños

27   *I*
Encounters
of your flesh and mine
continual clashing
arms
and legs
and successive kisses
and always your head
turning
and me with it

II
Gods
who test their strength
observe, in silence
sculptors their work
we
shaping our bodies
mounting with confidence
the steps

III

Montado sobre vos
yegüa mía
veo tus espaldas
anchas
moverse acompasadas
tirarme desde el centro;
un pedo
sólo un pedo al morir

III

Mounted on you
my mare
I see your broad
shoulders
heaving in rhythm
pulling me from the center;
a fart
just a fart when we come

28 Soy un gato blanco
peludo
con los ojos muy abiertos.
Sé las tretas del juego
una por una
y debajo de mi piel
escondido
se agazapa un instante

Estira el brazo
no temas;
es algo que siempre tarda

28   *I'm a white cat*

furry

with my eyes wide open.

I've got all the tricks

down pat

and hidden

under my skin

a moment ducks for cover

Stretch out your hand

don't worry:

it's something that always takes its time

DARÍO CANTON, the author of **Poamorio**, was born in Argentina in 1928. He is a graduate of the University of Buenos Aires in philosophy and letters and of the University of California at Berkeley in sociology. His published works of poetry include **El saga del peronismo** (1964), **Corrupción de la naranja** (1968), **Poamorio** (1969), **La mesa** (1972), **Poemas familiares** (1975), **Asemal** (1975-78) and **Abecedario Médico Canton** (1977). In 1983 he received a grant from the Social Science Research Council to study the relationship between occupation and voter behavior in Argentina's 1983 elections. His historical and sociological works include: **El parlamento argentino en épocas de cambio: 1890, 1916 y 1946** (1966), **Materiales para el estudio de la sociología política en la Argentina** (1968), **La política de los militares argentinos: 1900-1971** (1971), **Pequeño censo de 1927** (with José L. Moreno) (1971) and **Elecciones y partidos políticos en la Argentina** (1973). He has also written a textual analysis of the songs of the great Argentine tango composer, Carlos Gardel, **Gardel ¿a quién le cantás?** (1972).

DREW McCORD STROUD, the translator, was born in Arizona in 1944. He teaches Spanish at the University of Arizona in Tucson. He graduated from Harvard College in 1966. He is the author of an anthology on European migration to America, **The Minority Majority** (1974) and two books of poetry, **Lines Drawn Towards** (1980) and **The Hospitality of Circumstance** (1984). With S. J. Sigrist, he has translated **Night of the Milky Way Railroad** (1984), a short novel for children by Kenji Miyazawa. For several years he managed a small chamber orchestra, the Urban Philharmonic Society, directed by the noted Black American conductor, Darrold Hunt.

THEODOSIA ANDERSON, whose work "Titan" appears on the cover, is noted for her highly original creations composed of animal bones and painted artifacts, as well as for her enameled metal sculpture. A former student of Millard Sheets and Linford Donovan, she is the author of **Design Kerajanan Tangan**, published in Indonesia by the Asia Foundation.

SARU was founded in 1980 in the Year of the Monkey ("Saru" in Japanese). As the Society for the Advancement of Racial Unity, it is dedicated to the achievement of cultural understanding among the peoples of the Pacific Basin, in particular those who speak English, Spanish and Japanese.